BEASTS OF CHASE

ALSO BY ANDREW MACK

Weekend Revival

What the River Was

BEASTS

ANDREW MACK

OF

POEMS

CHASE

LOBLOLLY
PRESS
ASHEVILLE, NC

ASHEVILLE, NC

Copyright © 2025 by Andrew Mack

All rights reserved. No part of this publication may be reproduced, distributed, or transmitted in any form by any means, including photocopying, recording, or other electronic methods without the prior written permission of the author, except in the case of brief quotations embodied in reviews and certain other noncommercial uses permitted by copyright law. For permission requests, write to the publisher at loblolly.publishing@gmail.com.

PRESIDENT ROOSEVELT BEAR HUNTING, THE BEAR AT BAY, Creator unknown, from the Doris A. and Lawrence H. Budner Theodore Roosevelt Collection, DeGolyer Library, Southern Methodist University.

From HUNTING THE GRISLY AND OTHER SKETCHES; AN ACCOUNT OF THE BIG GAME OF THE UNITED STATES AND ITS CHASE WITH HORSE, HOUND, AND RIFLE. by Theodore Roosevelt. New York, London, G. P. Putnam's sons, 1909. Pdf. https://www.loc.gov/item/02001054/.

North Carolina Wildlife Resources Commission. North Carolina Black Bear Management Plan: 2012–2022. April 2012. Pdf. https://www.ncwildlife.gov/media/1428/download.

Cover & book design by Andrew Mack

Published by Loblolly Press
loblollypress.com
Instagram: @loblolly_press

ISBN: 979-8-9900730-7-4
Printed in the United States of America

First Printing, April 2024

For my sweet Penelope Mack—

and the bear who mistook my truck for a vending machine.

The Black Bear.

In the East it has always ranked second only to the deer among the beasts of chase. The bear and the buck were the staple objects of pursuit of all the old hunters.

Its meat is good and its fur often valuable; and in its chase there is much excitement, and occasionally a slight spice of danger.

Theodore Roosevelt

Hunting the Grisly & Other Sketches

CHESTNUT

I

Imported in the early 1900s for ornamental gardens, Asian Chestnut Trees, resistant to *cryphonectica parasitica*, but still carrying the pathogen, introduced Chestnut Blight to American Chestnuts causing one of the greatest ecological disasters of the 20th century; by 1940, nearly all Chestnuts had been eradicated.

II

Environmental pressures and habitat resilience: as Chestnuts died and as black bears were hunted they became more dependent on crops, garbage, cities, and towns, increasing conflicts between wildlife and humans. Black bears searching for food were hunted, poached, and culled by the state, to reduce conflict.

III

Hyperphagia:

In other words,

to live is to hunger.

FREQUENTLY ASKED QUESTIONS

Why are black bears so timid?

After the First Snow—
A big bear
Lying in wait, ambling across ridge lines
Late into the evening—
Is killed—a successful
Hunting trip—

▼

Why do black bears play?

A black bear
      Catching mice
and Chipmunks
      Turning over logs
and seeing what she finds
      Two cubs in tow
rolling.

▼

Do black bears hunt people?

Rarely. In reality, black bears only attack people when provoked, for example, in the same way any other mother might protect their children.

What does it mean to be extirpated?

Expansion Westward; Manifest Destiny; Monroe Doctrine; Roosevelt Corollary;

Divine Right; Annexing indigenous land; "Indian" Removal; Displacement;

Habitat Loss; Over hunting; Unregulated Progress; Fragmentation;

Local extinction.

▼

How do I stay safe around black bears?

Secure your garbage.

Maintain direct eye contact.

Speak firmly.

Do not run.

Do not play dead.

▼

How do black bears prepare for birth?

Like this: she moves   when the hunter steps into the clearing
near a den she has   prepared by layering pine needles, oak
leaves, spruce   bows inside a log hollowed
out by time,   by fungus and decay.
The hunter   follows as she leads
him away   through blackberry
brambles, small   briars scraping the
hunter's legs, a plethora of small scrapes, blood beading on skin,
sliding softly, staining the tops of white socks.

▼

Do bears smell?

Only sometimes;
blackberries and blueberries and raspberries
stuck in the corners of their mouths
and all along their face, an eternal syrup
of mast fruit kissed by
midsummer oak, and pine.

▼

Do black bears growl?

A black bear, in all of recorded history, has never once been heard growling.

Only a soft grunt often compared to the sound a dog makes when it has caught a scent,

Or a pig: snuffling earth for acorns or treasured truffles.

■

DEAD MEAT

Some   bear in the woods
    is up a tree, driven there
        by a pack of
           dogs—Their owners
yell   *Stay! Hold! Heel!*
    while they aim guns
                toward treetops.

Some bear in the woods
is dead,
                         was dangling,
                         for a moment—
                         like a leaf
                         in the fall. The bear

is dead weight
    an imprint of
    hundreds of pounds
    of acorns and
    berries eaten in
    a hyperphagic
    frenzy, preparing
    for the winter
    it will never see.

                         Some dog in the woods
                             has hip bones that could cut

hiker's calves, and now,
knowing his work
is complete, the dog
looks to the bear
and considers what
     he has done.
     What kind of work
     leaves behind
     this sense of dread?
     What kind of work
     lives in the flesh
     as grief,
      kill against all instinct?
Some   dog in the woods
  breaks free, runs,
    dew dripping along
     his torso
      leaves crashing
       underneath his feet,
gunshots   ringing in his ears,   and through the valley
               of his mountain,
    the ridge line echoing the sound
         of all these years,
   urging us toward the trees:
            warning us to run.

LIVING THINGS YOU KNOW

Branches split
like book spines.

The bear
descends into the
backyard pond,
paws dragging silt,
tearing the roots
loose.

The broken lining
leaks,
suffocates fish,
and precedes
environmental collapse
for wood frogs who
mate here in winter.

Except,
this year,
they have
been rescued by
our flood,
by rain
filling craters
left from tree fall.

Puddles
at first barren—
now full
of life.

COWARDICE

after   Scott   Ferry's   "Vessels"

radios scream through the hills / the static like something alive / cutting through trees / we walk on until we spot her / a dog ambling down the mountain / she arrives / thin as wire / she is hungry / ribs sharpened against skin / tail bones jut out like small mountains / she is thirsty / she eats hard boiled egg / lettuce / tomato / sandwich bread / drinks water from a ziploc bag bowl / she has been left out here or rather escaped / living off small streams / lampbugs / grubs / acorns / small creatures / she is wearing a collar and GPS tracker / antennae bouncing as she walks / searching for some signal from above / her breath drags behind us / we search for cell service to call the number on her collar / a man picks up / *what?* / *we have your dog* / silence / she's tied to us with p-cord now / around our wrists / cicadas scream through gently falling leaves / we cannot give her back to them / we won't / but they are waiting in ripped jeans and orange vests / hands fastened to their guns / *here* / we cut the cord / surrender / *take her* / we watch them while dust and trees swallow the road

CRAVEN COUNTY, 1998

"The current world record black bear was harvested in Craven County in 1998 and weighed 880 pounds."

History of Black Bears in North Carolina

Who knows
what will come from the hunt—
this gathering of men
in Craven County.

Leaves split and shatter underfoot.

They move in threes,
shoulders brushing,
rifles steady,
seeking the secret black bear
known only in myth
and tall tales as
the stranger.

How long
have these men
been hunting
these woods—
yearning
for something
to show
and tell.

SOFT MAST

The leaves have become impossibly thin.

The branches, bent at odd angles, escape their roots.

As if being eaten is reason enough to flee.

HUNTING SEASON

On Saturday mornings

I'm with their wives

   at Food Lion,

      examining produce,

         looking for something

good

to eat,

while the husbands

      are out hunting.

They don't

see I'm watching

     when they sneak a bite

of plum. Sugar

     against teeth, juice

         slipping down their chins

the flesh blooming

at the corner

  of their mouths,

testing for ripeness.

Then putting it back.

We see each other—

  their faces turn red.

I wink.

Grin.

  They hold my gaze,

knowing we've been caught

red-handed

  the day before Sunday.

BUZZING

I thought at first it was a hive.

I know they are common here, either hornets digging deep and unsettling earth, or honey bees storing combs in birch logs.

You can hear the buzzing only when you are directly on top of them, but this time the smell stung first—

This buck rotting; leg bones and flesh decay while flies hurriedly feast.

RHODODENDRON

Playful rays Bounce across Brown pupils
Stout snouts Emerge now Into a world
Filled with fire Until gray green Violet blue
Overtake orange And gold Petals fall
Like small bells, Gently ringing In the sky
Look up Blossoms rain

CROW

Crows perched

In a dead tree

Sound the alarm

As cubs

Skirt around trees

Like fog.

Deer, mice,

Other small mammals,

Alert,

Wait until they pass

Before going about the ordinary

Business of their lives.

THE BEAR

I

At first light, the sun bends across the dried riverbed, mud cracks—
a hard red skin indented with tracks: the soft splay of bear pads.

II

Moving south, the bear shifts her weight— two cubs weave between
her legs until the snap of a branch, nearby, and then the scent:
rust and pine sap; the sound of a stomach grumbling. She stiffens.

III

He raises his rifle slowly, the heavy pull of it against his
shoulder— *Down, down. Steady.* Like our fathers taught
us. A breath; the bear turns to face him. Sniffs the air.

There are some things older than hunger.

ACKNOWLEDGMENTS

First and foremost, to my husband, Garrison Mack — for his unflinching support, for making me book the several writing retreats required to put this thing together, and for helping me get back on track after the storm (and every day). I couldn't have written this without you.

To EA Wilcox — my chosen sibling and my first ever editor. More than just a sharp eye, you've helped me create a support network and a family that keeps my writing sustainable. Art doesn't happen without the time, support, and safety to create it — and you've been a part of facilitating all of that. Your guidance is always evident in my work. I'm endlessly grateful.

To Clint Bowman — a close friend and a generous editorial contributor to this collection. More than that, thank you for being there with me in the woods, for the conversations and quiet moments that became the backbone of these poems. This work carries the weight of those memories.

To Cheryl Whitehead — now a constant inspiration in my work. I cannot wait for your voice to take up the space it deserves in the world.

To Peter and Erin Maxeiner-Healy — for housing me as I wrote the bulk of this chapbook, for giving me the space and time to create. I'm so grateful for your generosity and friendship.

To Hudson Myracle — you are one of the people who saved me this past year. You are a true community member in every sense of the word. I'm so thankful for you.

To Sean Theodore Stewart — for cheering me on, for always being interested in my work, and for making me feel like what I create matters.

To the queer community — we're going through hell, and yet we survive. This collection is for you — for us.

PLAYLIST

Listen to the songs that inspired *Beasts of Chase*:

Bird of Paradise 🦅 Frazey Ford

Rain 🦅 Patty Griffin

The Tern 🦅 Beirut

Sagres 🦅 The Tallest Man On Earth

Environmental Anxiety 🦅 RAYE

Bored 🦅 Waxahatchee

I Don't Mind 🦅 Sturgill Simpson

All Things End 🦅 Hozier

Meet Me in the Woods 🦅 Lord Huron

September Song 🦅 Willie Nelson

LOBLOLLY PRESS

Loblolly Press is an independent press based out of Asheville, North Carolina that is dedicated to publishing contemporary poetry, short fiction, and novels from emerging and marginalized writers across the American South. Our goal is to publish writers with a distinctly Southern voice from communities and experiences not always represented in traditional publishing. We're striving to create a community of writers and readers who feel deeply connected to the work we publish because they can see themselves represented within it.

RECENT AND FORTHCOMING FROM LOBLOLLY PRESS

The Surfacing of Joy 🌰 Earl J. Wilcox (2023)

If Lost 🌰 Clint Bowman (2024)

Distant Relations 🌰 Cheryl Whitehead (2025)

The Computer Room 🌰 Emma Ensley (2025)

Habitats 🌰 Garrett Ashley (2026)

Book design and composition by Andrew Mack.

Editorial assistance from EA Wilcox & Clint Bowman.

Design assistance from Garrison Mack.

The headings and poems are set in Cormorant.

www.ingramcontent.com/pod-product-compliance
Lightning Source LLC
Chambersburg PA
CBHW052131030426
42337CB00028B/5121